My Life Matters

Compiled by Imagine Me LLC

BK Royston Publishing
P. O. Box 4321
Jeffersonville, IN 47131
502-802-5385
http://www.bkroystonpublishing.com
bkroystonpublishing@gmail.com

© Copyright – 2020

All Rights Reserved. No part of this book may be reproduced, stored in a retrieval system, or transmitted by any means without the written permission of the author.

Cover Design: BK Royston Publishing
Cover Photo: Shannon Drummond Photography LLC
shannondrummondphotography@gmail.com

ISBN-13: 978-1-951941-65-9

Printed in the United States of America

Foreword

The longer a person lives on Earth, the greater their opportunities for growth. The end of growth certainly marks the cessation of life. Because the principle purpose of life is to grow, whenever growth meets potential, the essence of life is actualized.

This is the sole justification upon which the matter of a life rests. When a human life has reached its time of declaration of intent to live fully, it accomplishes its promise. It is then that You fully understand the matter of your existence.

Translation: Your Life Matters! Who you are and who you shall become is being foretold in this time!

Standing upon the testimony of ***MY LIFE MATTERS*** you will be able to see the **M**agic and **Y**outh of life's possibilities. Your **L**IVING will be the **I**NSPIRATION that **F**ORTIFIES an **E**NERGETIC charge forward into that which has been predestined just for you! The **M**agnificence of what is being realized in **A**bundance of the living

TRUTH inside your gifted mind, body, and spirit is beyond sufficient **T**ranscription. From **E**verlasting to evermore and eternity, the **R**eign of your **S**ong shall be like the dew in the morning gently resting upon the power of your living story!

May your living resonate throughout the Universe bringing forth peace and blessings to you first and thereafter every life assigned to your destiny! Let us live like it matters because it does!

In service and humility,
Latascha L. Craig, MSSW, CSW, M.Ed.
CEO, Imagine Me, LLC

Table of Contents

Foreword	iii
Chloe Elliott	1
Noah Fields	7
Josiah T. Finley	13
Ron'Neal Flippins	21
Chris Hollingsworth	29
Kenzleigh T. LeFlore	37
Dewayne L. Richards	49
Karinton Smith	57
Sai'Vion D. Vaughn	67

My Life Matters
Chloe Elliott

"She overcame everything that was meant to destroy her."
Sylvester McNutt, III

My Life Matters
Chloe Elliott

My life matters because I am awesome, humble, and intelligent. My life matters because it will help the world one day in many ways. When I grow up, I want to be a pediatrician, which means I want to be a doctor for infants and children. I want to do this because I want kids to be healthy. I also want to know that I have been part of making sure kids live healthy lives.

My life also matters because I have so much to accomplish, both now and in my adult years. I have many skills that will help me make my dreams a reality and will make me successful. My life matters because God gave it to me. I am truly thankful and blessed to have been given a life. And the blessed life I have matters.

My life matters because I am a role model to many people younger than me, including my little brother and my younger cousins, who are trying to follow in the right direction. Even though I didn't choose to be the oldest, I am. And that means younger family members are watching what I do to help them grow. We have to do the right thing whether we want to or not, so that young ones don't think that wrong is right and right is wrong.

My life matters and God made me talented. Sometimes we have to remember we are special in our own way. For me, I am a good leader, a caring friend, a baker, a swimmer, and someone who gives good advice. On the flip side, there are things that are not my talents, such as singing and athleticism. But instead of focusing on what I am not, I shine through my God-given talents.

There are times when I have to remind myself that MY LIFE MATTERS. Sometimes, I can forget that truth. Sometimes when I forget, I can feel like an outsider in my friend circle because of my differences. But the great thing is my friends care about me, and they remind me that our differences are what makes us special. I am a firm believer that EVERYTHING happens for a reason! The family I belong to, the friends I have, and the path of my life. Everyone has a life that is different. So we must make it our own. We must make it count. We must make it matter.

It's almost like decorating a cake. For example, sometimes we borrow illustrations for cake design and decorating from other cake designers. But if we pay attention, the designs will never be exactly the same. The way I design it will still be different from others, no matter how closely it resembles the original. The design does not affect the taste. It is still a cake that can be enjoyed and will taste delicious. Even with being different, it is those differences that make our lives special and unique. This is why your life matters. This is why MY LIFE MATTERS!

My Life Matters
Noah Fields

"Find the good. It's all around you. Find it, showcase it, and you'll start believing in it."
                                    Jesse Owens

My Life Matters
Noah Fields

My life matters a lot, and people need to recognize that. God put me on this planet for a reason, and I intend to be the best person I can be while I am here. I am an African American, brown-skinned boy who is educated and great. I am gifted in math and science. I am a son, a big brother, a cousin, a student, a grandson, a nephew, a friend, and a child of God. My parents called me a prince who will grow up to be a king. My life matters.

My life matters because my generation is the future. When I grow up, I want to be an astronaut or an engineer for NASA. I want to go to space and learn about what's beyond our planet. I plan to attend the University of Louisville or Hampton University, an HBCU, to obtain my degree in engineering or aviation depending on which is better for me. There have been only eighteen African American astronauts. I want to be among those ranks. My life matters.

My life matters because I am Black. Black lives matter, period. Black people have been through a lot of adversity for many years, but that won't stop us. It cannot stop us. Some Black people are struggling in life because of the color of their skin. Lots of people are being shot and/or killed for having black or brown skin. I have hope that this can stop one day. Dr. Martin Luther King, Jr. said, "One day we will live in a nation where they will not be judged by the color of their skin, but by the content of their character." One day we will see his dream come true. My life matters!

    Yes, I am a young Black man, and my life matters. It matters first because I was made by God and then because I will be part of the people that change the world. President Barack Obama once stated, "Change will not come if we wait for some other person or some other time. We are the ones we've been waiting for. We are the change that we seek." I will be the change for our country, our world, and generations after me.

Thank you for reading and understanding that #MYLIFEMATTERS!

Sincerely,
Noah Fields

My Life Matters
Josiah T. Finley

"...usually hidden behind our fears are second chances waiting to be seized."
— Barry Allen, "The Flash"

My Life Matters
Josiah T. Finley

.......And thankfully, I have trusted people who tell me that every day. I believe them. However, the very people I grew up thinking were sworn protectors of this nation and the citizens of it are showing me that by their accounts, my life does not matter to them. I now suppose their actions have always carried that message, but my naïveté would not let me receive it. The system that proposes to educate me taught me that slavery, the fight for civil rights, and the oppression of people of color were things of the past. We have overcome, right? What it neglects to acknowledge is the new face of the regime and its longstanding plot to exterminate any reference to my existence. The injustice system and the miseducation system. People who look like me and experience life as I do continue to be targeted, hunted, and slaughtered like cattle to this very moment. So even while I slumber somewhat peacefully amidst my middle-class home life and neighborhood atmosphere protected under one nation, under God, with liberty and justice for all, some lie in wait to assure me of the value of my life to their cause.

But my hope is built on nothing less than my unending faith in the Creator of this Universe. So, while I may not be inherently rich, biologically Caucasian, or protected by militarized forces, I am too stubborn to believe their truth. I have lived a little longer than 15 years, and my hearing and vision are far too developed for me to give credit to their bigotry and hateful heart. I am a wiser being than I was when I first heard the "story." I know it for sure—MY LIFE MATTERS.

My life matters to me. My life matters to my family. My life matters to my friends. My life matters to my community. My life matters to my culture. My life matters to the future. My life is an opportunity. It is a chance for me to create change and to bear witness to the cause behind my name. Any disregard for my life or its importance is the deprivation of the possibilities my life offers to this world. Any judgment of my life's worth as less than necessary is the dismissal of the promise and purpose it brings to the advancement of humanity—

including people of all races, ethnicities, religions, genders, and sexual identities.

The attribution of my worth to the hue of my skin is a failure of personal intelligence. The attribution of my integrity to the dime-size experience with a minority generalized as the characterization of the majority is a failure of personal wisdom and insight. The persecution of my soul based on the imbalance of your self-worth is a failure of personal mortality. The prosecution of my life based on the illegitimacy of others is a failure of personal morality.

MY LIFE MATTERS because it came to be on purpose, and in spite of any weapon formed against it, it shall meet its purpose, because all things work together for the good of them who love

Him and are called according to His purpose. We are all connected—one to another. Every life, breath, and movement taken by one absolutely affects us all. So only because MY LIFE MATTERS, so does yours. And just because your life matters, so does mine.

The way that my life matters is the same way that yours does. I am an inhabitant of this perfectly formed, imperfectly led planet, just as you are.

And regardless of my gender, race, ethnicity, cultural or religious affiliation, sexual orientation, sensual preference, or choice of political party denomination, MY LIFE MATTERS.

I am: a divine creation of God, a son of mankind, a brother to others, a friend to many, and an enemy only to hatred. I am a leader, mentor, conqueror, caregiver, truth-seeker, and light-bearer. The matters of my life are actually anything but a small matter at all. These matters are **M**iracle-birthing, **A**mbition-driven, **T**ruth-breathing, **T**ransformational, **E**nergetically committed, **R**everently empathic, and **S**uccessfully astute.

In Peace,
Josiah T. Finley

My Life Matters
Ron'Neal Flippins

"If you can't fly then run,
if you can't run then walk,
if you can't walk then crawl,
but whatever you do you have to
keep moving forward."
                    Martin Luther King, Jr.

"Determined to succeed against the odds!"
                    Ron'Neal Flippins

My Life Matters
Ron'Neal Flippins

As a young, Black American male living in the middle of a nationwide fight for racial equality and justice, I have thought a lot about my own life and why it matters. Before the coronavirus crisis and the threat to our safety, I do not know that I ever thought much about the specific value of life. While spending so much time following the news of how this health crisis is costing people their lives and the deaths of people of color at the hands of others due to hatred, I began to think about how we spend our time living. Then, shortly thereafter, my city and others became involved in a social justice battle with the evil of racism. It was then that I realized that I am not only charged with proving my importance as a person because of my skin color, but I have to prove that my life is even worth being "permitted" to live. This has caused me to reflect on why my life is important and how I value myself.

My life matters because I am an intelligent, ambitious Black male with plans to succeed and change the world for better. It starts with me having a beautiful family that supports me and shows up for everything I do. Both my mother and my father love me, and I am important to them. My life matters to them and that matters to me. My parents enjoy spending time with me, and therefore, my life does not deserve to be taken from my family. My life matters because I have younger siblings that look up to me and follow what I do. I am responsible for being a good role model and big brother to my younger sister and my younger brother. My life matters to my grandparents, my aunts, uncles, cousins, and my friends. It matters because they know me as a good person that loves to have fun and participate in events. Family is important to my life and my life is important to my family. One day, I hope to make my family extremely proud by being successful in my career and my life.

  My life matters because I respect myself and I respect others. Therefore, I am not a part of carrying hate and racism forward to my generation. My life matters because I do not fall into stereotypes and

I am not a danger to others or society. My life matters because I respect the law, value my education, and take responsibility for making good decisions in school and in the community. My life matters because I volunteer and I take care of younger kids. My life matters because inside of me is a strong, independent thinker that is determined to become greater each day. My life matters because my skin color does not determine my worth, but instead makes me worth a lot.

My life is important to this world because I was born to add to it and be a part of subtracting from hatred of any kind toward other lives. My goals in life matter because they will impact the world and change lives. My goals will create

Ron Neal Flippins | 26

opportunities for other people and make them better. My goals will help my community rise above the negativity and have a voice that spreads peace. My life is full of goals. Those goals are a part of my purpose. My purpose is why I was born. And I was born because my purpose is important and necessary. Therefore, my life not only matters, but it is important. My life is necessary. And that matters for sure.

My Life Matters
Chris Hollingsworth

"Be the change that you wish to see in the world."
                                    Chris Hollingsworth

My Life Matters
Chris Hollingsworth

My life matters because I know I have a unique role to play that will help make a change. The reason I say this is because there are so many crazy things going on in the world right now. Just like many other people in the world today, I want police brutality, racism, and hatred to end. I believe that it is going to take what I have inside of me to help bring change in the world starting with kids my age.

I am a talented, 14-year-old African American boy, and I play the silver trumpet. I love a lot of different styles of music. I believe that music can heal pain in people all around the world. My life matters because I have this talent. If I continue to share my love for music with others, it can help bring people together. My dream is to play in front of a big audience filled with people of all colors. And because of my music, they can all be in one place together and get along.

Another reason why my life matters is because I want to continue to be a positive influence and a great role model for my 9-year-old brother. I also have lots of little cousins who look up to me, and there are not very many young people around them who are making good choices. I have so much more to offer and so much to add to my family. I have to be around to serve my purpose in life. I have many more lives to touch as I grow as a person. My life matters because

God created me and He placed inside of me a desire to learn, grow, and share what I learn with others. I recognize my responsibility to be an upstanding part of my community as well as inciting change around the world for all people.

    My life is special, important, necessary, and speaks highly of the love my family has for me. I am a miracle, and God thought enough of me to keep me living for the last 14 years. And I believe He will keep me around for many more because I know how to show love, kindness, and be at peace with others. My family makes sure that I am taken care of and that I feel supported and loved. This is the reason I try very hard to make sure others feel welcomed around me. My mom tells me that I have the gift of making new friends. The truth is I just know what it feels like to be the new person in a place where everyone else is familiar with one another and moving about quickly. I also know that when people do not feel welcomed, loved, or supported, they tend to become bullies. As a person targeted by a bully, I tried to understand why I was being treated this way. But my mom told me something very powerful: "Hurting people hurt other people." After she explained the message behind this statement, I was able to comprehend the pain of other people in a way that made me empathetic. I felt like helping others became a part of my life. I enjoy doing things to help others, and it makes me feel important. I get to be a part of sharing love with others! This is why my life matters!

My Life Matters
Kenzleigh T. LeFlore

"Always remember that someone is rooting for you, even if it doesn't seem like it."

Kenzleigh T. LeFlore

My Life Matters
Kenzleigh T. LeFlore

My name is Kenzleigh T. LeFlore and I believe that my life matters. My life is important because it has a great purpose. When I listen to my mother tell me about the beginnings of my life and how my birth happened much earlier than planned, it convinces me even more of the value of my life. Being born prematurely is a risk not only to the child, but also to the mother. I am sure my birth and life have purpose because I am a walking miracle that continues to defy the odds.

I deserve to live because I have a reason in this world. My dream of becoming a healthcare professional is important to the advancement and development of equality in the healthcare profession, and provision thereof. Specifically relating to the minority communities where many are underserved and overlooked. I understand that my life matters because I can be a world-changer and spread good to the less fortunate. I deserve to live a life full of excitement and adventures. I deserve to live a life filled with lessons derived from overcoming obstacles. My life matters because it will bless others. I desire to travel and view life from the perspective of other cultures. I desire to live out my dreams and have the opportunity to help others live theirs.

When you hear the sound of music, specifically orchestra, you are listening to melodies that give my life importance. I love to play and compose music. This love affair began in 6th grade, when I learned of someone who looked like me that knew so much about orchestra. This discovery is what truly prompted me to learn more about the double bass. Because of her influence, I have had the opportunity to participate in the Louisville Youth Orchestra, an honors orchestra at Eastern Kentucky University, and several music competitions. Working toward becoming an accomplished musician and being principal chair in a statewide orchestra group have helped me see that my life matters. It matters because it makes beautiful music that brings hope, peace, and happiness to others. Pushing myself as a musician has shown me that

I am strong, determined, resilient, and capable. Therefore, my life matters.

I am special, unique, and a beautiful blend of many cultures and experiences. I can command a stage as a pageant participant or as a member in the musical group. My talents are given to me to help others. I celebrate others and God celebrates me. I have learned to extract the good out of every situation, and I try to pass that on to bless others. The love I have in my heart is why I walk with dignity and pride in myself. Therefore, my life matters.

When I think about the blessing of my everyday life, it makes me feel special, loved, and like my life matters. I had the opportunity to participate in a pageant that celebrated the cultural experience of young ladies like me. This opportunity presented me with more than competition; it taught me how to persist with maturity and respect through adversity. It helped me to recognize the beauty that I possess inside and to present myself in all situations with dignity and pride. The pageant provided some new and inspiring friendships with other girls my age that enjoyed some of the same things I enjoy. These friendships helped me to embrace my culture and its relevance to my purpose in life. I was grateful for this experience because I attended a school where I felt excluded because my culture was not celebrated. I was a minority. I often felt like I did not fit in, and this caused me to seek out ways to fit in, which included trying to change the way I look so I could resemble the other girls, who were white. I tried to change the way I acted to be accepted. I can remember asking my mother to allow me to "straighten my hair like the other girls." At the time I did not know what that meant. As I got older, I realized that my natural hair was beautiful and that I did not need to have straight hair to be pretty or to be accepted by others. Just as I am, I am enough. My life matters.

My life matters because I am finally a freshman in high school. I have completed middle school and look forward to my high school experience at an amazing high school that will expose me to many opportunities for success. I accomplished being accepted for enrollment into one of the best high schools in the state of Kentucky. Even though I am nervous, I am excited about the new friends that will potentially become lifelong. Establishing friendships is a strength for me, and it adds to why my life matters.

I am looking forward to going to football games with my friends, going to high school prom, homecoming, getting my driver's license, and just experiencing all the joys that come with high school. I am also looking forward to trying out for the field hockey and swim teams. And, yes, I like archery too.

My life matters because I am excited for my future as a young adult. A few years ago, at summer camp, I was able to watch an open-heart surgery at the University of Louisville Hospital. That really sparked a flame in me to want to study medicine and become a surgeon. During the surgery, it was something about the way the doctors worked together to help save someone's life. Seeing the actual beating of the heart is amazing to me. I am completely fascinated with the entire process.

My life matters because I believe in my ability to be the person I was created to be from conception. I will be involved in changing the lives of others. Being admitted to a historically Black college or university is my aspiration. I want to experience a great education, be a part of the college community, make lifelong friends, and decorate my dorm room. I am excited about attending football games and just enjoying my college experience. I am looking forward to attending medical school and becoming a doctor. I want to become an amazing doctor that helps people during their worst moments.

Because the health care system operates with a huge disparity between the care that minorities receive and the care given to non-minorities, I plan to be a part of the solution to fix that problem. I want to make sure that people who look like me receive excellent medical care and treatment, with special attention to prescribed medications. I know that my life matters because I will be a part of ensuring that regardless of race, gender, financial means, or social background, all will be able to live healthily and enjoy a good quality of life.

    Even though I know I cannot carry the world on my shoulders, I plan to live my life to the fullest and create a legacy that will benefit generations to come. My name, Kenzleigh T. LeFlore, will be a part of history-making progress for my people because MY LIFE MATTERS!

My Life Matters
Dewayne L. Richards

"Be Yourself Cause Everyone Else is Taken."

                        Dewayne L. Richards

My Life Matters
Dewayne L. Richards

My name is Dewayne L. Richards, and I was born on October 5, 2008. I was born on a Sunday at 1:27 a.m. My mother always says that "God rested on the day I was born because he had worked so hard all week to bring me to life." When I was born, I weighed a whopping 3 pounds and 5 ounces, and life was already set to be hard. I had to stay in the hospital for 5 weeks because I could not breathe or eat on my own. Once I got out of the hospital, I was sick all the time and had several surgeries, so I believe I am supposed to be here, after conquering all of that. That alone should be enough to matter, right? But my story was just beginning! I am a young Black man and I am rare! People see me, and some feel threatened and some feel comfortable. Either way, at some point in their mind, I matter!

At 11 years old, I have mattered to so many people. I matter to God, my family, my friends, my doctors, my church, and my teachers; most of them have helped me to become better and do better in every area of my important life. My life matters because I have something to offer the world. Not just my city, but the world. I am important because I was born, and when I was born, I was born with purpose. I have not yet figured out my full purpose, but I know God has blessed me with several gifts and talents that I enjoy. I enjoy helping people, I love cooking, and I like to laugh. I don't want to say when I grow up, I am going to be a chef because I'm already a chef today, but I plan to become world-renowned as a Chef, introducing recipes and dishes as unique and special as I am. When I cook, I think about how people are going to enjoy the meals I make. I think about how my family will come together and celebrate the dish or dinner. I think about how people are going to delight in the flavors and spices of my food. Not only does my life matter, but my recipes matter too!

My mother always says, "Some things you just have to keep to yourself," and she may be right, but my voice needs to be heard. Every morning, I watch the news and hear what is going on in the world. Some of it I believe is true, but with some of it I just shake my head and refuse to believe as the truth. The news tells us about what is going on in the world around me. My life is my voice that matters because the world today is my future for tomorrow. My life is my voice that matters because I may have the cure for cancer through my recipes. My life is my voice that matters because through helping people I may change my neighborhood. My life is my voice that matters because when I sit at the table in a board room, I may have a point that changes laws. My life is my voice that matters because I have friends and family that I can speak for when no one else may hear them. My life is my voice, and that matters!

On that Sunday when God rested, and He admired His work, I believe He looked at me and said, "Dewayne, you matter, and you have a purpose!" God said, "Dewayne, you are Black and kissed by the sun, you matter!" He said, "You are a man, and I created you to lead, you matter!" He said, "You have great ideas, and they will all help my world, you matter! God said, "I made you in the image of me, and I will say I look good, you matter!" God made me because he loves me, and because the greatest person in the universe made me, MY LIFE MATTERS!!!

My Life Matters
Karinton Smith

**God is within her, she will not fall;
Psalm 46:5 (NIV)**

My Life Matters
Karinton Smith

A few days ago, my mom and I were talking, and she asked me to write an essay about why I matter. To be honest, I was not sure how or where to start because, to look at me, you would see a young lady that has it all together and is living a good life. This is why you should always be careful how you treat others because you never know what they are struggling to overcome. Sometimes a smile can hide the truth. All of my short life, ever since I can remember, I have dealt with trying to be the fun girl with a lot to offer. I tried to be this person because I thought it would guarantee me acceptance, love, and friendship. Truthfully, it has been exhausting because I constantly get told things like, "You are too loud," "Your grades need to improve," "You are so lazy," and asked, "Do you ever shut up?" Unfortunately, even though I knew differently, I came to accept those things as a natural part of friendship and how I should be treated.

My transition to middle school was not at all a good experience. Because I did not feel satisfied with who I was, I constantly compared myself to others and would even question God, asking "Why me?" I would listen to negative messages in my head about myself. Those negative messages told me things like I was too fat, I needed to stop eating, I needed to look like someone else, and that I am less than. Several nights, I would awaken at 2 a.m. feeling alone and as if I had no one to talk to about how I was feeling. I would wake up to those thoughts, realizing that I was alone in having them and then spending the next hour telling myself it will all be OK. I tried to convince myself that I am beautiful no matter what the thoughts said to me. As I have always been pretty sensitive as a person, I never talked about my feelings out loud to other people until the day of a fateful car ride with my mom. We were talking like normal and planning for the type of home we wanted to move into when, all of a sudden out of nowhere, my mom asked a stunning question. "You do understand that you matter, right? And you do understand why you matter, right?"

When my mom asked me that question, it left me wondering about what she meant in that moment and why she decided to ask at that time. Until then, I guess I never gave much thought to the importance of my life in an everyday sense. I knew I mattered to her and my family, but I never thought about why. During that car ride, I began to think about it, asking myself if I believe that my life matters. At first thought, I could not say yet with confidence. I never considered my talents and what I have to offer this world through the living of my life.

But my mom began to talk about why I mattered to other people in my life. She started to talk about how I changed my grandmother's life because she was in this dark hole after the death of my grandfather. She said that my grandmother needed someone to love her back to life. Then I came. My grandmother's life changed for the better. She smiles a lot and laughs a lot now. My mom reminded me about my friends and how they look up to me. We talked about my mom's only sibling, my Uncle Derek, and how he adored me from my first breath. Uncle Derek's life changed upon my arrival. He felt a sense of responsibility and protective love for me. We were extremely close, and I adored him as much as he adored me. I know he is in heaven looking down on me even now.

Then my mom said one thing that I will never forget. She said, "Karinton, you

matter to me because you saved my life."
I looked at her and wondered what she meant. She began to tell me that she was not making the best decisions in her life at the time, and she had asked God to help her become a better person. Not long after that request, she found out she was pregnant with me, and her life changed right before her eyes. Everything that she thought she loved could never compare to the love she now has for me. She said my dad was happy about my birth, and he could not wait to see my face. Tears fell down my face as I listened to my mom talk about me and what I had done for so many people that I did not even realize. I am a person that truly matters in the lives of so many people.

Since that night, when I begin to question whether I matter, I remember what my mom said and how God used her to share His love for me. I now realize that my life matters. I am deeply loved, a friend to many, a light in the life of others, and I bring joy to those who know me. I do matter, and I am proud to say that my pride in myself has grown to knowledge that I am strong, intelligent, beautiful, talented, fashionable, friendly, and funny. Since birth, I have been changing lives, and with the help of God, I will change the world for the better! This is why MY LIFE MATTERS!

My Life Matters
Sai'Vion D. Vaughn

"Act as if what you do makes a difference. IT DOES."
William James

My Life Matters
Sai'Vion D. Vaughn

Greetings WORLD!

I am Sai'Vion D. Vaughn, an 11-year-old young man who truly believes my life matters. I am certain my life is important because living my life means living my destiny. I have a part in changing the future for my generation. I plan to do so many things for the future. I believe the generation I am a part of can do anything we set our minds to doing! We all need to believe that about us. I am a young Black King and cannot be convinced otherwise. I believe that I will be successful when I become an adult. I believe this because I am striving for success now. From being unique, left-handed, well-read, talented, and a child of God, I know that I have much to contribute to this world. In my short life, I have lived in three different states in the country. Along with my parents and two brothers who are also Black Kings, I have lived in Kentucky, where I was born. I also have an older sister, a Black Queen, who loves me and encourages me to be my best. We moved to South Carolina and then to Seattle, Washington. I have met many different people, learned about different cultures, and experienced things that have shaped my life for success.

My life matters because I am special and unique. I am an excellent reader, mathematician, and I am really good at sports. I enjoy learning new things about many subjects and I enjoy researching information to arm myself with knowledge. There are times when I find myself wondering about how I will make my mark in the world and make a difference in the lives of others. Then I just look to my parents and family who always keep me involved in the culture of love and service to others and I am reminded of the importance of my life. My family has made education important, and they always support me and my brothers in everything we do. There are even times when I don't have a choice to participate. My parents insist because they know it will make me a better person. I love the way my entire family gets together to share in supporting one another. My grandparents, aunts, uncles, cousins, siblings, and even friends that are like family show up to let me know I am important to this world. This is the main reason why I believe I can achieve. I also feel like I am responsible for making sure I make my parents and family proud of the man I am becoming. We all need to know our life is important and that it matters. It is good to know it now, because I may struggle as I grow up, and counting the good in my life will help me remember why my life matters. Everyone needs to figure out why their life matters. As long as I believe in myself, I will become the professional basketball player and businessman I want to be when I grow up. And as long as I believe it, it does not matter what anyone else thinks. My life matters to me. That is what I will tell myself every day. MY LIFE DEFINITELY MATTERS!

Sai'Vion Vaughn

Made in the USA
Columbia, SC
21 April 2023